FOR MY
DAD

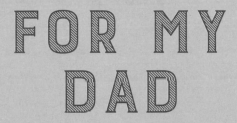

FOR MY DAD

INSPIRATIONS TO BRIGHTEN YOUR DAY

STERLING
New York

STERLING
New York

An Imprint of Sterling Publishing Co., Inc.
1166 Avenue of the Americas
New York, NY 10036

ISBN 978-1-4549-2884-3

Distributed in Canada by Sterling Publishing Co., Inc.
c/o Canadian Manda Group, 664 Annette Street
Toronto, Ontario M6S 2C8, Canada
Distributed in the United Kingdom by GMC Distribution Services
Castle Place, 166 High Street, Lewes, East Sussex BN7 1XU, England
Distributed in Australia by NewSouth Books
45 Beach Street, Coogee NSW 2034, Australia

For information about custom editions, special sales, and premium and corporate purchases,
please contact Sterling Special Sales at 800-805-5489 or specialsales@sterlingpublishing.com.

Manufactured in Canada

2 4 6 8 10 9 7 5 3 1

sterlingpublishing.com

Dedication

To My Father: A Book of Quotes
—By Wafa' Tarnowska and Adrian Gilbert

To my grandfather Ibrahim, who taught me how to love the earth.
—WT

FOREWORD

"DADDY." THIS IS THE NAME GIVEN TO THE MOST IMPORTANT MAN IN many children's lives, so not surprisingly it is one of the first words kids learn to say. But what do we mean when we utter it? Why not use a father's given name, such as John, David, or Mohammed? The answer to this simple question is a gateway to hidden spaces in our hearts. For "Dad" or "Daddy" is a not a name but a title—simultaneously intimate and abstract. To call this man "Daddy" is to define a relationship, a bond that goes beyond a mere name. For he is not just the source of half our genes but also our protector against what can seem like a hostile world.

It goes to follow that many children worship their dads as heroes. Dad looks after us materially and, if we are in trouble, comes immediately to our rescue. A dad's love, like that of a mother, is unconditional. He may be stern at times and get cross with us when we are naughty, but behind those angry words there is true love. More than anything, he wants us to succeed, to grow to maturity, and to fulfill our potential. He hopes that one day we may take on the role of mom or dad ourselves.

A dad has a natural inclination to encourage his children to become independent. He wants us to learn to take the bus to school instead of expecting to be driven. He is the one who removes the training wheels from the bicycle and challenges us to ride it without them. Never mind that we may take a tumble and graze a knee. A dad understands that if bicycles are ever to be of use to us, we must learn to ride them properly. He lets us take other risks too, such as climbing trees or playing football. He understands instinctively that it is only by taking these risks and suffering a few bruises that we develop the resilience needed to be responsible adults. Dad's love pushes us toward one day leaving the cozy nest to find our independence.

There is, of course, a price he may be forced to pay for all this "dadness." We may become frustrated with him for pushing us so hard, and sometimes it even seems like he might not have our best interests at heart. But in the end, we look back at all we've achieved and love him even more for his part in it. A wise dad understands us even when we doubt him, and he helps us develop a kingdom of our own just the same. And someday, if the burden shifts and we assume the role of parent ourselves, a son will be the dad and his own father a granddad, and both sons and daughters will remember the lessons Dad taught them when they're teaching their own children. In this way the light of love grows ever brighter, shining in mutual honor and respect between fathers and the sons and daughters who love them, spanning the generations.

WORLD FATHERS

Honor thy father and thy mother: that thy
days may be long upon the land which
the Lord thy God giveth thee.

—Exodus, Chapter 20, Verse 12 (The Bible)

When a father helps a son, both smile; but
when a son must help his father, both cry.

—Jewish Proverb

BEHOLD, CHILDREN ARE
A GIFT OF THE LORD,

THE FRUIT OF THE WOMB
IS A REWARD.

LIKE ARROWS IN THE
HAND OF A WARRIOR,

SO ARE THE CHILDREN
OF ONE'S YOUTH.

HOW BLESSED IS THE MAN WHOSE
QUIVER IS FULL OF THEM.

—Psalms 127:3–5 (The Bible)

Jesus saith unto him, I am the way,
the truth, and the life: no man
cometh unto the Father, but by me.

—John, Chapter 14, Verse 6 (The Bible)

God is a father, happiness is a stepfather.

—Jewish Proverb

When a son gives to his father,
they both weep.

—Jewish Proverb

One of life's greatest mysteries is how the
boy who wasn't good enough to marry
your daughter can be the father of the
smartest grandchild in the world.

—Jewish Proverb

Honor your father and your mother, as the Lord your God has commanded you, so that you may live long and that it may go well with you in the land the Lord your God is giving you.

—Deuteronomy, Chapter 5, Verse 16 (The Bible)

Blessed be the God and Father of our Lord Jesus Christ, the Father of mercies and God of all comfort.

—2 Corinthians, Chapter 1, Verse 3 (The Bible)

Train up a child in the way he should go— but be sure you go that way yourself.

Charles Spurgeon, British Preacher and Theologian (*The Treasury of David*)

It is easier for a father to have
children than for children
to have a real father.

—Pope John XXIII

The father of godly children has cause for joy.
What a pleasure to have children who are wise.

—Proverbs 23:24 (The Bible)

Father asked us what was God's noblest work. Anna said men, but I said babies. Men are often bad, but babies never are.

—Louisa May Alcott, American Novelist and Poet

For whosoever shall do the will of my Father who is in heaven, he is my brother, and sister, and mother.

—Matthew, Chapter 12, Verse 50 (The Bible)

Praise the Father who has purposed!
Praise the Son who all has done!
Praise the Spirit who transmitteth!
Praise the Three who work as one!

—Margaret Jenkins Harris, American Organist and Preacher

("Glory, Glory to the Father")

DEAR LORD AND FATHER OF MANKIND,

FORGIVE OUR FOOLISH WAYS!

—John Greenleaf Whittier, American Quaker Poet
("The Brewing of Soma," Adapted by Garrett Horder in the Hymn
"Dear Lord and Father of Mankind")

Eternal Father, strong to save,

Whose arm hath bound the restless wave,

Who bidd'st the mighty ocean deep

Its own appointed limits keep;

Oh, hear us when we cry to Thee,

For those in peril on the sea!

—William Whiting, Anglican Choirmaster ("Eternal Father, Strong to Save")

FATHER-LIKE, HE TENDS
AND SPARES US,

WELL OUR FEEBLE
FRAME HE KNOWS:

IN HIS HANDS HE
GENTLY BEARS US,

RESCUES US FROM
ALL OUR FOES.

—Henry Francis Lyte, Anglican Hymn Writer and Poet
("Praise My Soul, the King of Heaven")

THE GREATEST GIFT I EVER HAD
CAME FROM GOD; I CALL HIM DAD!

—Author Unknown

Our Father who art in heaven
Stay there
And we will stay on earth
Which is sometimes so pretty.

—Jacques Prévert, French Poet ("Pater Noster")

Anyone who loves their father or mother more than Me is not worthy of Me; anyone who loves their son or daughter more than Me is not worthy of Me.

—Matthew, Chapter 10, Verse 37 (The Bible)

Father! To God Himself we cannot
give a holier name.

—William Wordsworth, English Romantic Poet (*The Borderers*)

The truth was that Jay Gatsby, of West Egg, Long Island, sprang from his Platonic conception of himself. He was a son of God—a phrase which, if it means anything, means just that—and he must be about His Father's business, the service of a vast, vulgar and meretricious beauty.

—F. Scott Fitzgerald, American Novelist (*The Great Gatsby*)

HE CANNOT HAVE GOD FOR HIS FATHER WHO HAS NOT THE CHURCH FOR HIS MOTHER.

—Saint Cyprian, Bishop of Carthage

God is a good father to us all, and knows better than we do what is good for us. If we ask Him for something that is not good for us, He does not give it, but something better still, if only we will continue to pray earnestly and do not run away and lose our trust in Him.

—Johanna Spyri, Swiss Children's Author (*Heidi*)

As home from church we two did plod,
"Grandpa," said Rosy, "What is God?"
Seeking an answer to her mind,
This is the best that I could find . . .

God is the Iz-ness of our Cosmic Biz;
The high, the low, the near, the far,
The atom and the evening star;
The lark, the shark, the cloud, the clod,
The whole darned Universe—that's God. . . .

Said Rosy-kins: "Grandpa, how odd
Is your imagining of God.
To me he's always just appeared
A huge Grandfather with a beard."

—Robert William Service, British-Canadian Poet ("Rosy-Kins")

God's pleasure is in the pleasure of the father,
and God's displeasure is in the
displeasure of the father.

—The Hadith

The right of your father on you is that you should
know that it is he who brought you into existence,
and you are a branch of the tree of his life.

—Ali Ibn al Husayn, Shi'ite Muslim Leader

ONE DAY, ABU HURAIRAH SAW TWO MEN WALKING TOGETHER AND ENQUIRED OF THE YOUNGER ONE, "WHO IS THIS MAN TO YOU?" TO WHICH THE YOUNG MAN REPLIED, "HE IS MY FATHER." ABU HURAIRAH ADVISED HIM BY SAYING, "DO NOT CALL HIM BY HIS NAME, DO NOT WALK IN FRONT OF HIM, AND DO NOT SEAT YOURSELF BEFORE HE DOES."

—Abu Hurairah, Companion of the Prophet Muhammad

Your Lord hath decreed that ye worship none but Him and that ye be kind to parents. Whether one or both of them attain old age in thy life, say not to them a word of contempt, nor repel them, but address them in terms of honor. And out of kindness lower to them the wing of humility and say: "My Lord! Bestow on them Thy Mercy even as they cherished me in childhood."

—The Night Journey, Aura 17, Verses 23–24 (The Quran)

To support mother and father, to cherish wife
and children, and to be engaged in peaceful
occupation, this is the greatest blessing.

—The Buddha, Indian Philosopher

Karma is the mother and karma is the father.

—Burmese Proverb

God! Give us wisdom as a
father gives to his sons.
Guide us, O Much-invoked, in this path.
May we live in light.

—Rig Veda, 7.32.26

The Master said, "While a man's father
is alive, look at the bent of his will; when
his father is dead, look at his conduct. If
for three years he does not alter from the
way of his father, he may be called filial."

—Confucius, Chinese Philosopher
(*The Analects*, Translated by James Legge)

FAR FROM LOVE THE
HEAVENLY FATHER
LEADS THE CHOSEN CHILD,
OFTENER THROUGH
REALM OF BRIAR
THAN THE MEADOW
MILD, . . .

—Emily Dickinson, American Poet (*Poems*, LVI)

That learned Father,
who so firmly proves
The soul of man
immortal and divine,
And doth the several
offices define.

—Michael Drayton, Elizabethan Poet (*Idea*, Sonnet 12, "To the Soul")

He knelt, and leaning on the chair
He prayed and fell asleep;
And the moth-hour went from the fields,
And stars began to peep.

They slowly into millions grew,
And leaves shook in the wind;
And God covered the world with shade,
And whispered to mankind.

—William Butler Yeats, Irish Poet ("The Ballad of Father Gilligan")

ELDERLY
FATHERS

But Father John went up,
And Father John went down;
And he wore small holes in his Shoes,
And he wore large holes in his gown.

—William Butler Yeats, Irish Poet
("The Ballad of Father O'Hart")

YES, WHEN THE CROSSES WERE
CHALKED ON THE DOOR—
YES, WHEN THE TERRIBLE
DEAD-CART ROLLED!

EXCELLENT COURAGE OUR
FATHERS BORE—
NONE TOO LEARNED, BUT NOBLY BOLD
INTO THE FIGHT WENT OUR
FATHERS OF OLD.

—Rudyard Kipling, English Writer and Poet ("Our Fathers of Old")

Then, be good to us, stars above!
Then, be good to us, herbs below!
We are afflicted by what we can prove,
We are distracted by what we know.
So—ah, so!
Down from your heaven or
up from your mould,
Send us the hearts of
our Fathers of old!

—Rudyard Kipling, English Writer and Poet
("Our Fathers of Old")

The Mountain sat upon the Plain
In his tremendous Chair—
His observation omnifold,
His inquest, everywhere—

The Seasons played around his knees
Like Children round a sire—
Grandfather of the Days is He
Of Dawn, the Ancestor—

—Emily Dickinson, American Poet ("The Mountain")

"YOU ARE OLD, FATHER WILLIAM,"
THE YOUNG MAN SAID,

"AND YOUR HAIR HAS
BECOME VERY WHITE;

AND YET YOU INCESSANTLY
STAND ON YOUR HEAD—

DO YOU THINK, AT YOUR
AGE, IT IS RIGHT?"

—Lewis Carroll, English Writer and Mathematician

("You Are Old, Father William")

"Are you deaf, Father William!" the young man said,
"Did you hear what I told you just now?
Excuse me for shouting! Don't waggle your head
Like a blundering, sleepy old cow!"

—Lewis Carroll, English Writer and Mathematician
(Acrostic in the Style of "You Are Old, Father William")

Help your father
As he ages
And loses his strength
For it was he who sheltered you
And protected you from the storms.

—*The Khoisan Book of Wisdom*, of the Indigenous Population of Namibia

An old man goes there—who's now all white-haired—

With rapid steps and merry eyes, alone,

He smiles to us, and often calls with hand,

And leaves us with a gait, that is well-known.

—Aleksandr Blok, Russian Poet ("The Death of Grandfather")

Hasten thee, Kronos!
On with clattering trot!
Downhill goeth thy path;
Loathsome dizziness ever,
When thou delayest, assails me.
Quick, rattle along,
Over stock and stone let thy trot
Into life straightway lead!

—Johann Wolfgang von Goethe, German Writer and Poet
("To Father Kronos")

FATHERS
AND
SONS

MY FATHER DIDN'T TELL ME HOW TO LIVE; HE LIVED, AND LET ME WATCH HIM DO IT.

—Clarence Budington Kelland, American Writer

Sons have always a rebellious wish to be
disillusioned by that which charmed their fathers.

—Aldous Huxley, English Writer ("Vulgarity in Literature")

A man's desire for a son is usually nothing but
the wish to duplicate himself in order that such a
remarkable pattern may not be lost to the world.

—Helen Rowland, American Journalist and Humorist (*Reflections of a Bachelor Girl*)

The worst misfortune that can happen to an ordinary man is to have an extraordinary father.

—Austin O'Malley, Ophthalmologist and Professor of English Literature
(*Keystones of Thought*)

The father who does not teach his son his duties is as equally guilty as the son who neglects them.

—Confucius, Chinese Philosopher

He who is taught to live upon little owes more to his father's wisdom than he who has a great deal left him does to his father's care.

—William Penn, Founder of Pennsylvania (*Fruits of Solitude*)

SMALL BOYS BECOME
BIG MEN THROUGH
THE INFLUENCE OF
BIG MEN WHO CARE
ABOUT SMALL BOYS.

—Author Unknown

Gods and land of my fathers welcome me into your streets! And you, too, palace of my father, receive me well because I've come to you, sent by a god to cleanse you from all pollution. Don't send me away in shame but let me become a worthy ruler of my house and of my estate.

—Sophocles, Greek Dramatist (*Electra*)

He to whom God gives no sons, the devil gives nephews.

—Spanish Proverb

If they don't exchange a few words, father and son will never know one another.

—Indian Proverb

In my younger and more vulnerable years my father gave me some advice that I've been turning over in my mind ever since. "Whenever you feel like criticizing any one," he told me, "just remember that all the people in this world haven't had the advantages that you've had."

—F. Scott Fitzgerald, American Novelist (*The Great Gatsby*)

MY FATHER TAUGHT ME TO
WORK, BUT NOT TO LOVE IT.
I NEVER DID LIKE TO WORK,
AND I DON'T DENY IT. I'D
RATHER READ, TELL STORIES,
CRACK JOKES, TALK, LAUGH—
ANYTHING BUT WORK.

—Abraham Lincoln, Sixteenth American President

If you can talk with crowds and keep your virtue,

Or walk with Kings—nor lose the common touch,

If neither foes nor loving friends can hurt you,

If all men count with you, but none too much;

If you can fill the unforgiving minute

With sixty seconds' worth of distance run,

Yours is the Earth and everything that's in it,

And—which is more—you'll be a Man, my son!

—Rudyard Kipling, English Writer and Poet ("If")

Every father should remember that his son will one day follow his example instead of his advice.

—Charles F. Kettering, American Inventor

51

Listen, my son, to your father's instruction
and do not forsake your mother's teaching.
They are a garland to grace your head
and a chain to adorn your neck.

—Proverbs 1:8–9 (The Bible)

WHEN YOUR SON GROWS UP, BECOME HIS BROTHER.

—Arabic Proverb

A good son-in-law is like the acquisition of a new son; a bad one is like the loss of your daughter.

—Jewish Proverb

Whoever teaches his son teaches not only his son but also his son's son, and so on to the end of generations.

—Jewish Proverb

WHO LEAVES A SON ISN'T REALLY DEAD.

—Danish Proverb

My mother was fortune, my father generosity and bounty; I am joy, son of joy, son of joy, son of joy.

—Rumi, Sufi Poet

Oh, at home had I but stayed

'Prenticed to my father's trade,

Had I stuck to plane and adze,

I had not been lost, my lads.

—A. E. Housman, Classical Scholar and Poet ("The Carpenter's Son")

Farewell, thou child of my
right hand, and joy;
My sin was too much hope
of thee, lov'd boy.
Seven years thou wert lent
to me, and I thee pay,
Exacted by thy fate, on the just day.

—Ben Johnson, English Playwright and Poet ("On My First Son")

BID A STRONG GHOST
STAND AT THE HEAD
THAT MY MICHAEL MAY
SLEEP SOUND,
NOR CRY, NOR TURN IN THE BED
TILL HIS MORNING MEAL
COME ROUND.

—William Butler Yeats, Irish Poet ("A Prayer for My Son")

My young son asks me: Must I learn mathematics?
What is the use, I feel like saying. That two pieces
Of bread are more than one's about all you'll end up with.

My young son asks me: Must I learn French?
What is the use, I feel like saying. This State's collapsing.
And if you just rub your belly with your hand and
Groan, you'll be understood with little trouble.

My young son asks me: Must I learn history?
What is the use, I feel like saying. Learn to stick
Your head in the earth, and maybe you'll still survive.

Yes, learn mathematics, I tell him.
Learn your French, learn your history!

—Bertolt Brecht, German Poet and Playwright ("My Young Son Asks Me")

I'm leaving, Pater. Good–bye to you!
God bless you, Mater! I'll write to you!
I wouldn't be impolite to you,
But, Brother, you are a hound!

—Rudyard Kipling, English Writer and Poet ("The Prodigal Son")

I wish thee all thy
mother's graces,
Thy father's fortunes,
and his places.
I wish thee friends,
and one at court,
Not to build on, but support.

—Richard Corbet, English Poet (To His Son, Vincent Corbet)

I must not let my boy Dick down,
Knight of the air.
With wings of light he won renown
Then crashed somewhere.
To fly to France from London town
I do not dare.

—Robert William Service, British-Canadian Poet ("My Son")

Though coward I,

Let me revere till life be done

My hero son.

—Robert William Service, British-Canadian Poet ("My Son")

You don't have to deserve your mother's love. You have to deserve your father's. He is more particular. . . . The father is always a Republican towards his son, and his mother's always a Democrat.

—Robert Frost, American Poet (Interview in *Writers at Work*)

O DEAREST, DEAREST BOY! MY HEART

FOR BETTER LORE WOULD SELDOM YEARN,

COULD I BUT TEACH THE HUNDREDTH PART

OF WHAT FROM THEE I LEARN.

—William Wordsworth, English Romantic Poet ("Anecdote for Fathers")

OUR FATHERS ALL WERE POOR, POORER OUR FATHERS' FATHERS; BEYOND, WE DARE NOT LOOK. WE, THE SONS, KEEP STORE.

—Edwin Muir, Scottish Poet ("The Fathers")

Snug at the club two fathers sat,

Gross, goggle-eyed, and full of chat.

One of them said: "My eldest lad

Writes cheery letters from Bagdad.

But Arthur's getting all the fun

At Arras with his nine-inch gun."

"Yes," wheezed the other, "that's the luck!

My boy's quite broken-hearted, stuck

In England training all this year.

Still, if there's truth in what we hear,

The Huns intend to ask for more

Before they bolt across the Rhine."

I watched them toddle through the door,

These impotent old friends of mine.

—Siegfried Sassoon, English Poet ("The Fathers")

Good fathers make good sons.

—Albanian Proverb

Many a good father has but a bad son.

—Vietnamese Proverb

One father is enough to govern one hundred
sons, but not a hundred sons one father.

—Romanian Proverb

The father buys, the son lives big, the grandchild sells, and his son begs.

—Romanian Proverb

Less good than they say for the sons of men is the drinking often of ale: for the more they drink, the less can they think and keep a watch over their wits.

—Norse Proverb

If you know his father and grandfather you may trust his son.

—Moroccan Proverb

THE ENEMY OF A FATHER WILL NEVER BE FRIENDS OF HIS SON.

—Kurdish Proverb

If you love your son, let him travel.

—Japanese Proverb

Till age six, your son is your master; until ten he's
your servant; until sixteen, a wonderful adviser; from
then on, he's either your friend or your enemy.

—Jewish Proverb

If a father does not cultivate, the
son does not inherit land.

— Congolese Proverb

A son is a son till he gets him a wife, but a
daughter's a daughter the rest of your life.

—English Proverb

The dragon has nine sons, each
different from the others.

—Chinese Proverb

It is easier for the son to ask
from the father than for the
father to ask from the son.

—Bengali Proverb

As the baker, so the buns;
as the father, so the sons.

—Albanian Proverb

Lime and lime without manure makes
the father rich and the son poor.

—Albanian Proverb

When a father praises his
son, he flatters himself.

—American Proverb

Easier to rule a nation than a son.

—Chinese Proverb

Gambling is the son of avarice
and the father of despair.

—French Proverb

Treat your superior as a father, your equal
as a brother, and your inferior as a son.

—Persian Proverb

One son is no son, two sons is no son, but three sons is a son.

—Russian Proverb

Gambling sire, gambling son.

—Portuguese Proverb

Henry James once defined life as that predicament which precedes death, and certainly nobody owes you a debt of honor or gratitude for getting him into that predicament. But a child does owe his father a debt, if Dad, having gotten him into this peck of trouble, takes off his coat and buckles down to the job of showing his son how best to crash through it.

—Clarence Budington Kelland, American Writer

It is not flesh and blood but the heart which makes us fathers and sons.

—Friedrich Schiller, German Poet and Philosopher (*The Robbers*)

Dad, you're someone to look up to no matter how tall I've grown.

—Author Unknown

One night a father overheard his son pray: "Dear God, make me the kind of man my daddy is." Later that night, the father prayed, "Dear God, make me the kind of man my son wants me to be."

—Author Unknown

SORROW FOR THE DEATH
OF A FATHER LASTS
SIX MONTHS; SORROW
FOR A MOTHER, A
YEAR; SORROW FOR A
WIFE, UNTIL ANOTHER
WIFE; SORROW FOR
A SON, FOREVER.

—Indian Proverb

A son is like a lopped off branch. As a falcon, he comes when he wills and goes where he lists.

—Ivan Turgenev, Russian Novelist (*Fathers and Sons*)

It always seems to the brothers and the father that their brother or son didn't marry the right person.

—Anton Chekhov, Russian Doctor and Playwright

My mother and father are the only people on the whole planet for whom I will never begrudge a thing. Should I achieve great things, it is the work of their hands; they are splendid people and their absolute love of their children places them above the highest praise. It cloaks all of their shortcomings, shortcomings that may have resulted from a difficult life.

—Anton Chekhov, Russian Doctor and Playwright (A Letter to His Cousin)

I had an inheritance from my father;
it was the moon and the sun. And though
I roam all over the world, the
spending of it's never done.

—Ernest Hemingway, American Novelist (*For Whom the Bell Tolls*)

The successful man tells his son to profit by his father's good fortune, and the failure tells his son to profit by his father's mistakes.

—F. Scott Fitzgerald, American Novelist (*The Beautiful and Damned*)

Toil on, son, and do not lose heart or hope. Let nothing you dismay. You are not utterly forsaken. I, too, am here—here in the darkness waiting, here attentive, here approving of your labor and your dream.

—Thomas Wolfe, American Novelist (*You Can't Go Home Again*)

The idea of bringing someone into the world fills me with horror. I would curse myself if I were a father. A son of mine! Oh no, no, no! May my entire flesh perish and may I transmit to no one the aggravations and the disgrace of existence.

—Gustave Flaubert, French Novelist (A Letter to Louise Colet)

DON'T HOLD YOUR
PARENTS UP TO
CONTEMPT. AFTER
ALL, YOU ARE THEIR
SON, AND IT IS JUST
POSSIBLE THAT YOU
MAY TAKE AFTER THEM.

—Evelyn Waugh, British Novelist and Journalist

"My father ain't in Europe; my father's in a better place than Europe." Winterbourne imagined for a moment that this was the manner in which the child had been taught to intimate that Mr. Miller had been removed to the sphere of celestial reward. But Randolph immediately added, "My father's in Schenectady."

—Henry James, American Author (*Daisy Miller*)

Dearest Father,
You asked me recently why I maintain that I am afraid of you. As usual, I was unable to think of any answer to your question, partly for the very reason that I am afraid of you, and partly because an explanation of the grounds for this fear would mean going into far more details than I could even approximately keep in mind while talking. And if I now try to give you an answer in writing, it will still be very incomplete . . .

—Franz Kafka, German-Language Novelist Born in Prague
(A Letter to His Father)

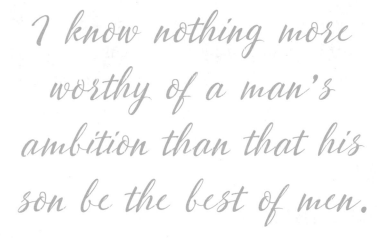

I know nothing more worthy of a man's ambition than that his son be the best of men.

—Plato, Greek Philosopher

To assert that the son of a slave is born a slave is to assert that he is not born a man.

Jean-Jacques Rousseau, French Philosopher (*The Social Contract*)

How pleasant it is for a father to sit at his child's board. It is like an aged man reclining under the shadow of an oak which he has planted.

—Sir Walter Scott, Scottish Novelist and Poet (Journal Entry)

The first step, my son, which one makes in the world, is the one on which depends the rest of our days.

—Voltaire, French Writer and Philosopher (*The Indiscrete*)

Teach your children poetry; it opens the mind, lends grace to wisdom and makes the heroic virtues hereditary.

—Sir Walter Scott, Scottish Novelist and Poet

My father was frightened of his mother; I was frightened of my father, and I am damned well going to see to it that my children are frightened of me.

—George V, King of Great Britain and Ireland

A WISE SON MAKETH A GLAD FATHER: BUT A FOOLISH SON IS THE HEAVINESS OF HIS MOTHER.

—Proverbs 10:1 (The Bible)

My mother groaned! My father wept.

Into the dangerous world I leapt:

Helpless, naked, piping loud;

Like a fiend hid in a cloud.

—William Blake, English Poet ("Infant Sorrow")

The father of a saint,
the son of a sinner.

—Spanish Proverb

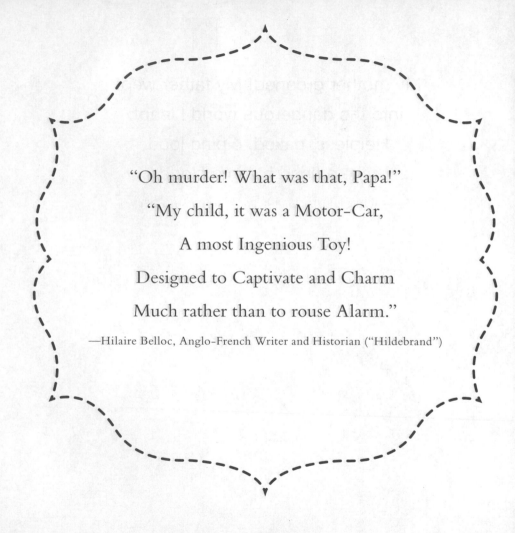

"Oh murder! What was that, Papa!"

"My child, it was a Motor-Car,

A most Ingenious Toy!

Designed to Captivate and Charm

Much rather than to rouse Alarm."

—Hilaire Belloc, Anglo-French Writer and Historian ("Hildebrand")

BE STILL, BE STILL,
WHAT CAN BE SAID?
MY FATHER SANG THAT SONG,
BUT TIME AMENDS OLD WRONG,
ALL THAT IS FINISHED,
LET IT FADE.

—William Butler Yeats, Irish Poet ("Three Marching Songs")

My father was a farmer upon
the Carrick border, O,

And carefully he bred me in
decency and order, O;

He bade me act a manly part,
though I had ne'er a farthing, O;

For without an honest manly heart,
no man was worth regarding, O.

—Robert Burns, National Poet of Scotland ("My Father Was a Farmer")

Father, where do the days all go?

Far, far. Each runs and races

No one can catch them, they leave no trace

Far, far. Whither, none may know.

—Ludvig Holstein, Danish Poet

("Father, Where Do the Wild Swans Go?")

The boy Alexander understands his
father to be a famous lawyer.

The leather law books of Alexander's
father fill a room like hay in a barn.

Alexander has asked his father to let him build a
house like bricklayers build, a house with walls
and roofs made of big leather law books.

—Carl Sandburg, American Poet and Writer ("Boy and Father")

Father, father, where
are you going
O do not walk so fast.
Speak father, speak
to your little boy
Or else I shall be lost.

—William Blake, English Poet ("The Little Boy Lost")

Come with me then, my son;
Thine eyes are wide for truth:
And I will give thee memories,
And thou shalt give me youth.

—Sir Ronald Ross, British Medical Doctor ("The Father")

Us boys ain't scared o' Pa so much
He only makes a noise,
An' says he never did see such
Onmanageable boys.

—James W. Foley, American Poet ("We Ain't Scared o' Pa")

THERE WAS A LOT OF WONDERS DONE WHEN MY PAW WAS A BOY; HOW GRANDPA MUST HAVE LOVED HIS SON, WHEN MY PAW WAS A BOY!

—Samuel Ellsworth Kiser, American Author and Journalist
("When My Paw Was a Boy")

Pop took me to the circus 'cause it disappoints me so
To have to stay at home, although
he doesn't care to go;
He's seen it all so many times,
the wagons and the tents,
The cages of wild animals and herds of elephants. . . .
Then by and by we're home again,
and Mamma wants to know
What kind of circus was it, and Pop
said, "The same old show,"
And said he'd seen it all before and all the reason he
Had stayed and seen it all 'cause it's all so new to me.

—James W. Foley, American Poet ("A Story of Self-Sacrifice")

My Pop is always buying books:
So that Mom says his study looks
Just like an old bookstore.
The book shelves are so full and tall
They hide the paper on the wall, . . .
Once, when I asked him why he got
So many books, he said, "Why not?"
I've puzzled over that a lot.

—Ralph Bergengren, American Satirist and Children's Poet ("Book Lover")

HENRY BLAKE'S FATHER
GOES FISHING WITH HIM,

AND GOES IN THE CREEK SO'S
TO TEACH HIM TO SWIM,

HE TALKS TO HIM JUST LIKE
THEY'RE AWFUL CLOSE CHUMS

AND SOMETIMES AT NIGHT
HE HELPS HENRY DO SUMS.

—James W. Foley, American Poet ("An Unusual Chum")

I honored, loved and respected him and he
Gave me his love as pay!
I pass it onto that boy of mine
And hope and dream and pray . . . he may
Honor and love, respect, obey
His father in a better, nobler way
Than I did mine.

—D. G. Bechers, American Poet ("What My Father Was to Me")

The whiskey on your breath
Could make a small boy dizzy;
But I hung on like death:
Such waltzing was not easy.

—Theodore Roethke, American Poet ("My Papa's Waltz")

In conversation father can
Do many wondrous things;
He's built upon a wiser plan
Than presidents or kings.
He knows the Ins and outs of each
And every deep transaction;
We look to him for theories,
But look to ma for action.

—Edgar Albert Guest, American Poet ("What Father Knows")

"IN MY YOUTH," SAID HIS
FATHER, "I TOOK TO THE LAW,

AND ARGUED EACH CASE
WITH MY WIFE;

AND THE MUSCULAR STRENGTH,
WHICH IT GAVE TO MY JAW,

HAS LASTED THE REST
OF MY LIFE."

—Lewis Carroll, English Writer and Mathematician
("You Are Old, Father William")

my father moved through dooms of love
through sames of am through haves of give,
singing each morning out of each night
my father moved through depths of height.

—E. E. Cummings, American Poet ("My Father Moved Through Dooms of Love")

Every old man I see
Reminds me of my father
When he had fallen in love with death.

—Patrick Kavanagh, Irish Poet and Novelist ("Memory of My Father")

WITH MY FATHER
I WOULD WATCH DAWN
OVER GREEN FIELDS.

—Kobayashi Issa, Japanese Poet and Buddhist ("With My Father")

Come up from the fields, father,
here's a letter from our Pete,

And come to the front door mother,
here's a letter from thy dear son.

—Walt Whitman, American Poet and Journalist
("Come Up from the Fields, Father")

Everything I ever learnt as a small boy came from my father, and I never found anything he ever told me to be wrong or worthless. The simple lessons he taught me are as sharp and clear in my mind as if I had heard them only yesterday.

—Richard Llewellyn, English Novelist ("How Green Was My Valley")

Diogenes struck the father when the son swore.

—Robert Burton, English Scholar (*The Anatomy of Melancholy*)

"Eat at my table," said the king; "eat and drink, my son, even as pleaseth thee; but let it be at my table, and not with dissolute companions."

—The Talmud

Be careful to leave your sons well instructed rather than rich, for the hopes of the instructed are better than the wealth of the ignorant.

—Epictetus, Greek Stoic Philosopher

A DEAD FATHER'S COUNSEL, A WISE SON HEEDETH.

—Esaias Tegnér, Swedish Poet

Oh child, may you be happier than your
father, but in all other respects alike.
And then you would not be bad.

—Sophocles, Greek Dramatist

I came from the Father and entered the world. In
turn, I will leave the world and go to the Father.

—John, Chapter 16, Verse 28 (The Bible)

It is a wise child that knows
his own father.

—William Shakespeare, English Playwright
(*The Merchant of Venice*)

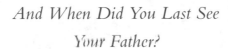

*And When Did You Last See
Your Father?*

—William Frederick Yeames, British Painter
(Title of a Painting)

ULYSSES IS SON TO LAERTES, BUT HE IS FATHER TO TELEMACHUS, HUSBAND TO PENELOPE, LOVER OF CALYPSO, COMPANION IN ARMS OF THE GREEK WARRIORS AROUND TROY, AND KING OF ITHACA. HE WAS SUBJECTED TO MANY TRIALS, BUT WITH WISDOM AND COURAGE CAME THROUGH THEM ALL . . . HE IS A COMPLETE MAN AS WELL, A GOOD MAN.

—James Joyce, Irish Writer (From Frank Budgen's Conversations with Joyce)

Happy am I that have a man so bold
That dares do justice on my proper son;
And not less happy, having such a son
That would deliver up his greatness so
Into the hands of justice.

—William Shakespeare, English Playwright (*Henry IV*)

PROVERBS
ABOUT
FATHERS

The fathers ate the cranberries and the children are left with the aftertaste.

—Russian Proverb

EARTHQUAKES, THUNDERBOLTS, FIRES, FATHERS.

—Japanese Proverb

SUCCESS HAS MANY FATHERS, BUT FAILURE IS AN ORPHAN.

—Albanian Proverb

Victory has a hundred fathers and defeat is an orphan.

—Chinese Proverb

At someone's funeral we weep for our own mothers and fathers.

—Tshi Proverb

They are happy, the free men that have their fathers.

—Bantu Proverb

You can buy everything, except
a father and a mother.

—Indian Proverb

FRIENDSHIP REMINDS US OF FATHERS, LOVE OF MOTHERS.

—Malagasy Proverb

When you follow in the path of your father, you learn to walk like him.

—Ghanaian Proverb

Few are like father, no one is like mother.

—Icelandic Proverb

A merry life forgets father and mother.

—French Proverb

The wish is the father of the deed.

—American Proverb

THE CHILD IS THE FATHER OF THE MAN.

—American Proverb

One father can feed seven children, but
seven children cannot feed one father.

—Cameroonian Proverb

FATHERS
AND
DAUGHTERS

A girl without a mother
is like a mountain with no
paths; a girl without a
father is like a mountain
with no streams.

—Kurdish Proverb

With my very own hands
I laid my little daughter
to rest because she is
of my very flesh,

Thus am I constrained to
submit to the rule of parting,
so that my hand is now empty
and contains nothing.

—Ibn 'Arabi, Andalusian Poet ("Diwan," Translated by Ralph Austin)

My daughter caught sight of me and cried out. "O Mother, there is Daddy!" Then her mother looked and saw me in the distance. Zainab went on calling. "There's my daddy! There's my daddy!" Then one of her uncles called to me and when I came to her she laughed and threw her arms round me shouting, "Daddy! Daddy!"

—Ibn 'Arabi, Andalusian Poet ("Futūhāt," Translated by Ralph Austin)

Don't worry about popular opinion

Don't worry about dolls

Don't worry about the past

Don't worry about the future

Don't worry about growing up

Don't worry about anybody getting ahead of you

Don't worry about triumph

Don't worry about failure unless it
comes through your own fault

Don't worry about mosquitoes

Don't worry about flies

Don't worry about insects in general

Don't worry about parents

Don't worry about boys

Don't worry about disappointments

Don't worry about pleasures

Don't worry about satisfactions.

—F. Scott Fitzgerald, American Novelist (Letter to His Daughter)

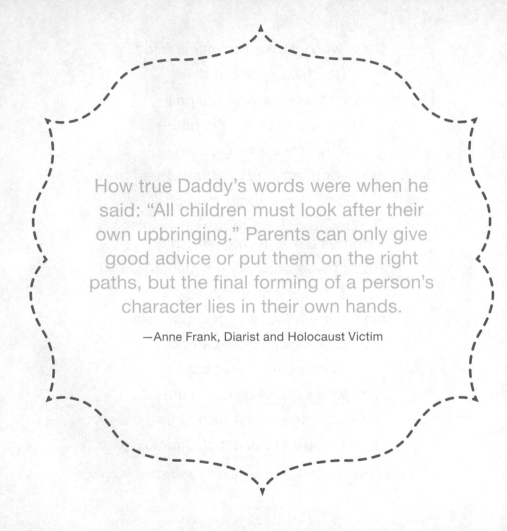

How true Daddy's words were when he said: "All children must look after their own upbringing." Parents can only give good advice or put them on the right paths, but the final forming of a person's character lies in their own hands.

—Anne Frank, Diarist and Holocaust Victim

They say that from the instant he lays eyes on her, a father adores his daughter. Whoever she grows up to be, she is always to him that little girl in pigtails. She makes him feel like Christmas. In exchange, he makes a secret promise not to see the awkwardness of her teenage years, the mistakes she makes, or the secrets she keeps.

—Author Unknown

TO A FATHER GROWING OLD NOTHING IS DEARER THAN A DAUGHTER.

—Euripides, Greek Dramatist

Every woman may not be queen to her husband
but every daughter is a princess to her father.

—Portuguese Proverb

As the lily among thorns, so is my
love among the daughters.

—Song of Solomon, Chapter 2, Verse 2 (The Bible)

And thou shalt in thy daughter see, this picture once, resembled thee.

—Ambrose Philips, English Poet and Politician

Balt Van Tassel was an easy indulgent soul; he loved his daughter better even than his pipe, and, like a reasonable man and an excellent father, let her have her way in everything.

—Washington Irving, American Writer (*The Legend of Sleepy Hollow*)

There is no kind of affection purely angelic as of a father to a daughter. In love to our wives, there is desire, to our sons, ambition; but to our daughters there is something which there are no words to express.

—Joseph Addison, English Essayist

A father is someone that

holds your hand at the fair,

Makes sure you do what your mother says,

Holds back your hair when you are sick,

Brushes that hair when it is tangled
because mother is too busy,

Lets you eat ice cream for breakfast,

But only when mother is away.

He walks you down the aisle

And tells you everything is going to be ok.

—Author Unknown

FIRST A DAUGHTER, THEN A SON, AND THE FAMILY'S WELL BEGUN.

—Albanian Proverb

One good daughter is worth seven sons.

—Russian Proverb

For, Annie, you see, her father
was not the man to save,

Hadn't a head to manage, and
drank himself into his grave.

—Lord Alfred Tennyson, Poet Laureate of Great Britain
and Ireland ("The Grandmother")

A DAYLIGHT MOON HUNG UP
IN THE WESTERN SKY, BALD WHITE.
LIKE PAPA'S FACE, SAID SISTER,
HURLING THE WHITE BALL FORTH.

—Delmore Schwartz, American Poet and Writer
("The Ballad of the Children of the Czar")

Lord grant that thou may aye inherit

Thy mither's person, grace, an' merit,

An' thy poor, worthless daddy's spirit.

—Robert Burns, National Poet of Scotland
("A Poet's Welcome to His Love-Begotten Daughter")

Daddy, I have had to kill you.

You died before I had time——

Marble-heavy, a bag full of God,

Ghastly statue with one gray toe

Big as a Frisco seal.

—Sylvia Plath, American Poet ("Daddy")

If I've killed one man, I've killed two—
The vampire who said he was you
And drank my blood for a year,
Seven years, if you want to know.
Daddy, you can lie back now.

—Sylvia Plath, American Poet ("Daddy")

Daddy, daddy, you bastard, I'm through.

—Sylvia Plath, American Poet ("Daddy")

When daddy shaves and lets me stand and look.

I like it better than a picture book.

He pulls such lovely faces all the time

Like funny people in a pantomime.

—Rose Fyleman, English Writer and Poet ("Fairies and Friends")

Run, little Bess and ope the door,
And do not let him wait.
Shout, baby, shout! And clap thy hands,
For father on the threshold stands.

—Mary Howitt, English Poet and Author ("Father Is Coming")

The vision of her girlhood glinted by;
And how the father through
their garden stray'd
And child with children, play'd.

—Francis Turner Palgrave, British Critic and Poet
("Margaret Roper's Vision of Her Father, Sir Thomas More")

She hears me strike the board and say
That she is under ban
Of all good men and women,
Being mentioned with a man
That has the worst of all bad names;
And thereupon replies
That his hair is beautiful,
Cold as the March wind his eyes.

—William Butler Yeats, Irish Poet ("Father and Child")

Down in the fields all prospers well,

But now from the fields come father, come at the daughter's call,

And come to the entry mother, to the front door come right away.

—Walt Whitman, American Poet and Journalist
("Come Up from the Fields, Father")

You fathers will understand. You have a little girl. She looks up to you. You're her oracle. You're her hero. And then the day comes when she gets her first permanent wave and goes to her first real party, and from that day on, you're in a constant state of panic.

—Frances Goodrich and Albert Hackett, Hollywood Screenwriters
(*Father of the Bride*)

I can lock her in her room. I can take her to Italy. But the only way I can keep her is to let her go away. I'm too old and too tired to run after her anymore. It's your turn. And a terrible time she'll give you!

—Melville Shavelson and Jack Rose, Hollywood Screenwriters (*Houseboat*)

You are my life!
Without you, what would
I have on earth?
Ah, my daughter!

—Francesco Maria Piave, Italian Librettist (Libretto for the Opera *Rigoletto*)

Bless your daughter, O my father—
in heaven above, near my mother,
I shall pray for you evermore.

—Francesco Maria Piave, Italian Librettist (Libretto for the Opera *Rigoletto*)

THE DEAR FATHER WOULD WITH HIS DAUGHTER SPEAK, COMMANDS, TENDS SERVICE.

—William Shakespeare, English Playwright (*King Lear*)

Come forth, old man—Thy daughter's side
Is now the fitting place for thee:
When time has quell'd the oak's bold pride,
The youthful tendril yet may hide,
The ruins of the parent tree.

—Sir Walter Scott, Scottish Novelist and Poet ("Woodstock")

NEW
FATHERS

TO BE A SUCCESSFUL FATHER, THERE'S ONE ABSOLUTE RULE: WHEN YOU HAVE A KID, DON'T LOOK AT IT FOR THE FIRST TWO YEARS.

—Ernest Hemingway, American Novelist

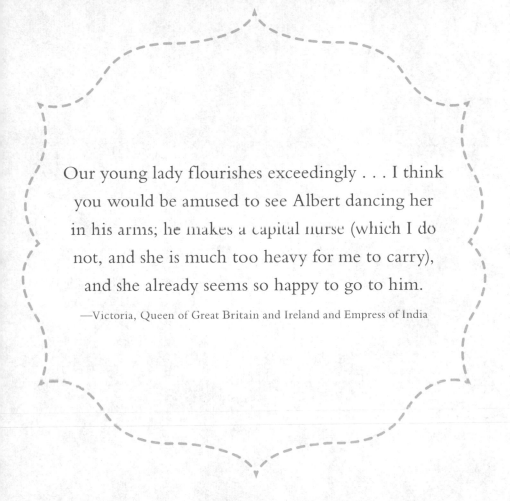

Our young lady flourishes exceedingly . . . I think
you would be amused to see Albert dancing her
in his arms; he makes a capital nurse (which I do
not, and she is much too heavy for me to carry),
and she already seems so happy to go to him.

—Victoria, Queen of Great Britain and Ireland and Empress of India

A man can deceive his fiancée or his mistress as much as he likes and, in the eyes of a woman he loves, an ass may pass for a philosopher. But a daughter is a different matter.

—Anton Chekhov, Russian Doctor and Playwright (Letter to Madame Avilov)

IF YOU'D EVER HAD A GROWN-UP
DAUGHTER YOU'D KNOW THAT
BY COMPARISON A BUCKING
STEER IS EASY TO MANAGE.
AND AS TO KNOWING WHAT
GOES ON INSIDE HER—WELL,
IT'S MUCH BETTER TO PRETEND
YOU'RE THE SIMPLE, INNOCENT
OLD FOOL SHE ALMOST
CERTAINLY TAKES YOU FOR.

—Somerset Maugham, British Playwright and Novelist (*The Razor's Edge*)

My unhealthy affection for my second daughter has waned. Now I despise all my seven children equally.

—Evelyn Waugh, British Novelist and Journalist

I have a wife and two daughters, my wife's health is delicate and so on and so on, and if I had to begin life all over again I would not marry. . . . No, no!

—Anton Chekhov, Russian Doctor and Playwright (*The Three Sisters*)

Greetings my father. I'll call you father because I can recognize my father in you. You wouldn't be surprised to know that within the one day, I both hated you and loved you more than anyone else!

—Sophocles, Greek Dramatist (*Electra*)

GRANDFATHERS

Perfect love sometimes does not come
until the first grandchild.

—Welsh Proverb

A grandfather is a babysitter who watches
the kids instead of the television.

—Author Unknown

Grandfather–grandchild relationships are simple.
Grandpas are short on criticism and long on love.

—Author Unknown

❖

A grandfather is a little bit parent, a little
bit teacher, and a little bit best friend.

—Author Unknown

You've got to do your own growing, no matter how tall your grandfather was.

—Irish Saying

A grandparent is old on the outside but young on the inside.

—Author Unknown

Don't correct an older man. Encourage him, as you would your own father. Treat younger men as you would your own brother, and treat older women as you would your own mother. Show the same respect to younger women that you would to your sister.

—1 Timothy, Chapter 5, Verses 1–2 (The Bible)

GRANDFATHERS ARE FOR LOVING AND FIXING THINGS.

—Author Unknown

My grandfather used to say: Life is astoundingly short. To me, looking back over it, life seems so foreshortened that I scarcely understand, for instance, how a young man can decide to ride over to the next village without being afraid that—not to mention accidents—even the span of a normal happy life may fall far short of the time needed for such a journey.

—Franz Kafka, German-Language Novelist Born in Prague ("The Next Village")

Because I would rather be with my grandfather
on Alp than anywhere on earth.

—Johanna Spyri, Swiss Children's Author (*Heidi*)

A grandfather is someone with silver
in his hair and gold in his heart.

—Author Unknown

Not long after, and while it was still twilight, the grandfather also went to bed, for he was up every morning at sunrise, and the sun came climbing up over the mountains at a very early hour during these summer months. The wind grew so tempestuous during the night, and blew in such gusts against the walls, that the hut trembled and the old beams groaned and creaked. . . . In the middle of the night the old man got up. "The child will be frightened," he murmured half aloud. He mounted the ladder and went and stood by the child's bed.

—Johanna Spyri, Swiss Children's Author (*Heidi*)

Are you the Earl? I'm your grandson, you know, that Mr. Havisham brought. I'm Lord Fauntleroy.

—Frances Hodgson Burnett, British-American Novelist (*Little Lord Fauntleroy*)

More precious than our children are the children of our children.

—Egyptian Proverb

If any one had told me I could be fond of a child, I should not have believed them. I always detested children—my own more than the rest. I am fond of this one and he is fond of me. I am not popular; I never was. But he is fond of me. He was never afraid of me—he always trusted me. He would have filled my place better than I have filled it. I know that. He would have been an honor to the name.

—Frances Hodgson Burnett, British-American Novelist (*Little Lord Fauntleroy*)

The feet of the rats
scribble on the door sills;
the hieroglyphs of the rat footprints
chatter the pedigrees of the rats
and babble of the blood
and gabble of the breed
of the grandfathers and the
great-grandfathers
of the rats.

—Carl Sandburg, American Poet and Writer
("Four Preludes to Playthings of the Wind")

What would your Great Grandfather who
Was Aide-de-Camp to General Brue,
And lost a leg at Waterloo,
And Quatre-Bras and Ligny too!
And died at Trafalgar!
What would he have remarked to hear
His Young Descendant shriek with fear,
Because he happened to be near
A Harmless Motor-Car!

—Hilaire Belloc, Anglo-French Writer and Historian ("Hildebrand")

This widow's father and grandfather
were born in Shantung.

Although they never held high office,
their fame spread far and wide.

I remember when they carried
on animated discussions

With other scholars by the city gate.

The listeners were so crowded that
their sweat fell like rain.

—Li Qingzhao, Chinese Writer and Poet ("To Lord Hu")

Old fathers,
great-grandfathers,
Rise as kindred should.
If ever lover's loneliness
Came where you stood,
Pray that Heaven protect us
That protect your blood.

—William Butler Yeats, Irish Poet ("Love's Loneliness")

Grandfather sang it under the gallows:

"Hear, gentlemen, ladies,
and all mankind:

Money is good and a girl
might be better,

But good strong blows are
delights to the mind."

There, standing on the cart,

He sang it from his heart.

—William Butler Yeats, Irish Poet ("Three Marching Songs")

The First. My great-grandfather
spoke to Edmund Burke

In Grattan's house.

The Second. My great-grandfather shared

A pot-house bench with Oliver Goldsmith once.

The Third. My great-grandfather's
father talked of music,

Drank tar-water with the Bishop of Cloyne.

—William Butler Yeats, Irish Poet ("The Seven Sages")

It's certain that my luck is broken,
That rambling jailbird Billy said;
Before nightfall I'll pick a pocket
And snug it in a feather bed.
I cannot find the peace of home
On great-grandfather's battered tomb.

—William Butler Yeats, Irish Poet
("Under the Round Tower")

. . . Snow grew overnight on the roofs of the houses like a pure and grandfather moss, minutely ivied the walls and settled on the postman, opening the gate, like a dumb, numb thunder-storm of white, torn Christmas cards.

—Dylan Thomas, Welsh Poet (*A Child's Christmas in Wales*)

Great Grandfather was ninety-nine
And so it was our one dread,
That though his health was superfine
He'd fail to make the hundred.

—Robert William Service, British-Canadian Poet ("The Centenarian")

Once I saw mountains angry,
And ranged in battle-front.
Against them stood a little man;
Aye, he was no bigger than my finger.
I laughed, and spoke to one near me,
"Will he prevail?"
"Surely," replied this other;
"His grandfather's beat them many times."
Then did I see much virtue in grandfathers—
At least, for the little man
Who stood against the mountains.

—Stephen Crane, American Poet (XXII in *The Black Riders and Other Lines*)

And then I watched a painter chap,
Grey—haired, a grandfather, mayhap,
Who daubed with delicate caress
As if in love with loveliness,
And looked at me with vague surmise,
The joy of beauty in his eyes.

—Robert William Service, British-Canadian Poet ("Tranquility")

Wading through a dark muddy street
I'm going to the shadow play
Ramazan night
a paper lantern leading the way
maybe nothing like this ever happened
maybe I read it somewhere an eight-year-old boy
going to the shadow play
Ramazan night in Istanbul holding
his grandfather's hand
his grandfather has on a fez and
is wearing the fur coat
with a sable collar over his robe
and there's a lantern in the servant's hand
and I can't contain myself for joy.

—Nâzım Hikmet, Turkish Poet and Playwright ("Things I Didn't Know I Loved")

The old Jimmy Woodser comes into the bar

Unwelcomed, unnoticed, unknown,

Too old and too odd to be drunk with, by far;

So he glides to the end where the lunch baskets are

And they say that he tipples alone.

His frockcoat is green and the nap is no more,

And his hat is not quite at its best;

He wears the peaked collar our grandfathers wore,

The black-ribbon tie that was legal of yore,

And the coat buttoned over his breast.

—Henry Lawson, Australian Poet ("The Old Jimmy Woodser")

BUT I DREAMED, AS HE TASTED
HIS "BITTER" TO-NIGHT

AND THE LIGHTS IN THE
BAR-ROOM GREW DIM,

THAT THE SHADES OF THE FRIENDS
OF THAT OTHER DAY'S LIGHT,

AND OF GIRLS THAT WERE BRIGHT
IN OUR GRANDFATHERS' SIGHT,

LIFTED SHADOWY GLASSES TO HIM.

—Henry Lawson, Australian Poet ("The Old Jimmy Woodser")

Pipit sate upright in her chair

Some distance from where I was sitting;

Views of the Oxford Colleges

Lay on the table, with the knitting.

Daguerreotypes and silhouettes,

Here grandfather and great great aunts,

Supported on the mantelpiece

An Invitation to the Dance.

—T. S. Eliot, British Poet ("A Cooking Egg")

I am my father's father,
You are your children's guilt.

In history's pity and terror
The child is Aeneas again;

Troy is in the nursery,
The rocking horse is on fire.

Child labor! The child must carry
His fathers on his back.

—Delmore Schwartz, American Poet and Writer
("The Ballad of the Children of the Czar")

THE INNOCENT ARE OVERTAKEN,

THEY ARE NOT INNOCENT.

THEY ARE THEIR FATHER'S FATHERS,

THE PAST IS INEVITABLE.

—Delmore Schwartz, American Poet and Writer
("The Ballad of the Children of the Czar")

Grandfather, grandfather gray,

Give me molasses, or I'll throw you away.

—Amy Lowell, American Poet ("A Roxbury Garden")

I can only remember a Russian peasant who told me his grandfather warned him: If you ride too good a horse you will not take the straight road to town.

—Carl Sandburg, American Poet and Writer
("Put Off the Wedding Five Times and Nobody Comes to It")

My grandfather said to me
as we sat on the wagon seat,
"Be sure to remember to always
speak to everyone you meet."

—Elisabeth Bishop, American Poet ("Manners")

My first advice on how *not* to grow old would be to choose your ancestors carefully. Although both my parents died young, I have done well in this respect as regards my other ancestors. My maternal grandfather, it is true, was cut off in the flower of his youth, at the age of sixty-seven, but my other three grandparents all lived to be over eighty.

—Bertrand Russell, English Philosopher
(*Portraits from Memory and Other Essays*)

DEARLY
DEPARTED
FATHERS

O YE WHOSE CHEEK THE
TEAR OF PITY STAINS,

DRAW NEAR WITH PIOUS
REV'RENCE, AND ATTEND!

HERE LIE THE LOVING
HUSBAND'S DEAR REMAINS,

THE TENDER FATHER, AND
THE GEN'ROUS FRIEND;

—Robert Burns, National Poet of Scotland (Epitaph on the Author's Father)

Thou gav'st the riches of thy streams,
The lordship o'er thy waves,
The region of thine infant dreams,
And of thy fathers' graves.

—Lydia Huntley Sigourney, American Poet
("The Indian's Welcome to the Pilgrim Fathers")

Lightly we tread o'er the grassy mounds,
Where the bones of our fathers rest;
They are gone to the happy hunting grounds,
They're gone, and they are blest!
Strong in the battle-fleet in the chase,
And wise when the old men met;
Their spirits dwell in the pleasant place,
But their sons remember yet.

—Charles Mackay, Scottish Poet and Writer ("The Graves of Our Fathers")

Such a dreadful death, such a pitiful death, father,
and yet, and yet, you've only got me! Only from me
do you receive your due of pity and a song of loss.

—Sophocles, Greek Dramatist (*Electra*)

God is Dead! Heaven is empty—

Weep, children, you no longer have a father.

—Gérard de Nerval, French Poet ("Le Christ aux Oliviers")

Those who have never had a father can at any rate never know the sweets of losing one. To most men the death of his father is a new lease of life.

—Samuel Butler, English Satirical Writer

Men sooner forget the death of their father than the loss of their patrimony.

—Niccolò Machiavelli, Italian Diplomat and Writer (*The Prince*)

I was ten when they buried you.

At twenty I tried to die

And get back, back, back to you.

I thought even the
bones would do.

But they pulled me
out of the sack,

And they stuck me
together with glue.

—Sylvia Plath, American Poet ("Daddy")

For I remember a quarrel I had
with your father, my dear,

All for a slanderous story, that cost me many a tear.

I mean your grandfather, Annie:
it cost me a world of woe,

Seventy years ago, my darling, seventy years ago.

—Lord Alfred Tennyson, Poet Laureate of Great Britain and Ireland
("The Grandmother")

This people's virtue yet so fruitful was

Of virtuous nephews that posterity

Striving in power their grandfathers to pass.

—Joachim du Bellay, French Poet ("Ruins of Rome," Translated by Edmund Spenser)

I CANNOT THINK THAT
YOU HAVE GONE AWAY,
YOU LOVED THE EARTH—AND
LIFE LIT UP YOUR EYES,
AND FLICKERED IN YOUR SMILE
THAT WOULD SURMISE
DEATH AS A SONG, A
POEM OR A PLAY.

—Iris Tree, English Poet, Actress, and Artists' Model ("To My Father")

Farewell, great spirit,
without fear of flaw,

Thy life was love and
liberty thy law,

And truth thy pure
imperishable goal.

—Sarojini Naidu, Indian Freedom Fighter and Poet
("In Salutation to My Father's Spirit")

One can't carry one's father's
corpse about everywhere.

—Guillaume Apollinaire, French Poet (*The Cubist Painters*)

He no longer breathes . . . his
limbs are cold. My father!

Beloved father! I'm fainting! I'm dying!

— Lorenzo da Ponte, Italian Librettist and Poet (Libretto for the Opera *Don Giovanni*)

My father is gone wild into his grave,
For in his tomb lie my affections,
And with his spirit, sadly I survive

—William Shakespeare, English Playwright (*Henry IV*)

But the father answered never a word,
A frozen corpse was he.

—Henry Wadsworth Longfellow, American Poet
("The Wreck of the Hesperus")

TO EVERY MAN UPON
THIS EARTH
DEATH COMETH SOON OR LATE.
AND HOW CAN MAN DIE BETTER
THAN FACING FEARFUL ODDS,
FOR THE ASHES OF HIS FATHERS,
AND THE TEMPLES OF HIS GODS?

—Baron Thomas Babington Macaulay, British Poet and Essayist ("Horatius")

FATHERHOOD

To her the name of father was another name for love.

—Fanny Fern, Journalist and Children's Author

A father carries pictures where his money used to be.

—Author Unknown

That is the thankless position of the father in the family—the provider for all, and the enemy of all.

—Johan August Strindberg, Swedish Playwright and Painter

I cannot think of any need in childhood as strong as the need for a father's protection.

—Sigmund Freud, Austrian Psychoanalyst

The heart of a father is the masterpiece of nature.

—Abbé Prévost d'Exiles, French Novelist

"Honor thy father and thy mother" stands written among the three laws of most revered righteousness.

—Aeschylus, Greek Dramatist

A dad is someone who
wants to catch you before you fall
but instead picks you up,
brushes you off,
and lets you try again.

A dad is someone who
wants to keep you from making mistakes
but instead lets you find your own way,
even though his heart breaks in silence
when you get hurt.

A dad is someone who
holds you when you cry,
scolds you when you break the rules,
shines with pride when you succeed,
and has faith in you even when you fail.

—Author Unknown

THE KIND UNCLES AND AUNTS OF THE RACE ARE MORE ESTEEMED THAN ITS TRUE SPIRITUAL FATHERS AND MOTHERS.

—Henry David Thoreau, American Philosopher (*Walden*)

The fundamental defect of fathers is that they want their children to be a credit to them.

—Bertrand Russell, English Philosopher ("Freedom Versus Authority in Education")

Wonderful tales had our fathers of old—
Wonderful tales of the herbs and the stars—
The Sun was Lord of the Marigold,
Basil and Rocket belonged to Mars. . . .
Wonderful little, when all is said,
Wonderful little our fathers knew.
Half their remedies cured you dead—
Most of their teaching was quite untrue.

—Rudyard Kipling, English Writer and Poet
("Our Fathers of Old")

How shall a man escape from his ancestors, or
draw off from his veins the black drop which
he drew from his father's or mother's life?

—Ralph Waldo Emerson, American Essayist ("The Conduct of Life")

TWO LITTLE GIRLS, ON THEIR WAY HOME FROM SUNDAY SCHOOL, WERE SOLEMNLY DISCUSSING THE LESSON. "DO YOU BELIEVE THERE IS A DEVIL?" ASKED ONE. "NO," SAID THE OTHER PROMPTLY. "IT'S LIKE SANTA CLAUS: IT'S YOUR FATHER."

—Author Unknown

Blessed indeed is the man who hears many gentle voices call him father!

—Lydia M. Child, American Writer and Abolitionist (*Philothea: A Grecian Romance*)

One father is more than a hundred schoolmasters.

—George Herbert, Welsh Poet and Anglican Priest

By profession I am a soldier and take pride in that fact. But I am prouder— infinitely prouder—to be a father. A soldier destroys in order to build; the father only builds, never destroys.

—Douglas MacArthur, American General

Govern a family as you would cook a very small fish: very gently.

—Chinese Proverb

No man should bring children into the world who is unwilling to persevere to the end in their nature and education.

—Plato, Greek Philosopher (*Crito*)

For just as poets are fond of their own poems, and fathers of their own children, so money-makers become devoted to money, not only because, like other people, they find it useful, but because it's their own creation.

—Plato, Greek Philosopher (*The Republic*)

❖

The fathers have eaten sour grapes, and the children's teeth are on edge.

—Ezekiel, Chapter 18, Verse 2 (The Bible)

O WHA MY BABIE-
CLOUTS WILL BUY?
O WHA WILL TENT
ME WHEN I CRY?
WHA WILL KISS ME
WHERE I LIE?
THE RANTIN' DOG,
THE DADDIE O'T.

—Robert Burns, National Poet of Scotland
("The Rantin' Dog, The Daddie O't")

Nay, but our children in our midst, what else
but our hearts are they, walking on the ground?
If but the breeze blow harsh on one of them
my eye says no to slumber all night long.

—Hittan Ibn al-Mu'alla of Tayyi, Arab Poet
("Parental Affection," Translated by Sir Charles James Lyall)

Let us dry our tears now laddie,

Let us put aside our woes,

Let us go and talk to daddy,

For I'm sure that daddy knows.

—James W. Foley, American Poet ("Daddy Knows")

So we ain't scared o' Pa at all

Although he thinks we are,

But when we hear Ma come an' call

No difference how far—

We are away, we answer quick.

—James W. Foley, American Poet ("We Ain't Scared o' Pa")

ONLY A DAD, BUT HE
GIVES HIS ALL
TO SMOOTH THE WAY FOR
HIS CHILDREN SMALL,
DOING, WITH COURAGE
STERN AND GRIM,
THE DEEDS THAT HIS
FATHER DID FOR HIM.

—Edgar A. Guest, American Poet ("Only a Dad")

My father was a tall man
and yet the ripened rye

Would come above his shoulder,
the spears shot up so high.

My father was a tall man
and yet the tasseled corn

Would hide him when he cut
the stalks upon a frosty morn.

—Jessie B. Rittenhouse, American Literary Critic and Poet ("My Father")

You rhymed like Lear for us when we were small.

Our walks with you were full of things mysterious

Made magic by your twinkle and half-drawl,

Because we could not tell if you were serious.

—William Rose Benét, American Poet, Writer, and Editor ("To My Father")

YOU KNOW YOUR DAD
AS A BIG, BIG, MAN;
A MARVELOUS BEING
THAT'S MOST LIKE GOD—
A BEING BUILT ON A
SPLENDID PLAN
WHO HOLDS THE WORLD
AT HIS BECK AND NOD.

—Strickland Gillilan, American Poet and Humorist ("Your Dad")

He does not feel the cold, not he,

His heart it is so warm;

For father's heart is stout and true

As ever human bosom knew.

—Mary Howitt, English Poet and Author
("Father Is Coming")

If I when my wife is sleeping
and the baby and Kathleen
are sleeping
and the sun is a flame-white disc
in silken mists
above shining trees,
if I in my north room
dance naked, grotesquely
before my mirror
waving my shirt round my head
and singing softly to myself:
"I am lonely, lonely.
I was born to be lonely,
I am best so!"

—William Carlos Williams, American Poet ("Danse Russe")

And the sins of the fathers shall be
visited upon the heads of the children,
even unto the third and fourth
generation of them that hate me.

—Stephen Crane, American Poet
("And the Sins of the Fathers Shall Be")

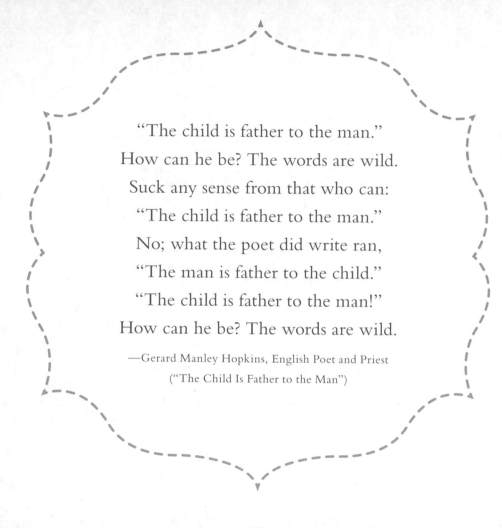

"The child is father to the man."
How can he be? The words are wild.
Suck any sense from that who can:
"The child is father to the man."
No; what the poet did write ran,
"The man is father to the child."
"The child is father to the man!"
How can he be? The words are wild.

—Gerard Manley Hopkins, English Poet and Priest
("The Child Is Father to the Man")

He never made a fortune, or a noise

In the world where men are

seeking after fame;

But he had a healthy brood

of girls and boys

Who loved the very ground

on which he trod.

—Ella Wheeler Wilcox, American Author and Poet ("Father")

Death will be my wedding, children, and glory.

—Euripides, Greek Dramatist ("Iphigenia in Aulis")

Becoming a father is easy enough, but
being one can be very rough.

—Wilhelm Busch, German Painter and Poet

No fathers or mothers think their own children ugly; and this self-deceit is yet stronger with respect to the offspring of the mind.

—Miguel de Cervantes, Spanish Writer (*Don Quixote*)

◈

Our father's love is to the bastard Edmund As to the legitimate: fine word,—legitimate!

—William Shakespeare, English Playwright (*King Lear*)

**Fathers that wear rags
Do make their children blind;
But fathers that bear bags
Shall see their children kind.**

—William Shakespeare, English Playwright (*King Lear*)

Don't go into Mr. McGregor's garden: your Father had an accident there; he was put in a pie by Mrs. McGregor.

—Beatrix Potter, English Writer and Illustrator (*The Tale of Peter Rabbit*)

"Papa is a preferable mode of address," observed
Mrs. General. "Father is rather vulgar, my dear. The
word Papa, besides, gives a pretty form to the lips.
Papa, potatoes, poultry, prunes and prism, are all
very good words for the lips: especially prunes and
prism. You will find it serviceable, in the formation
of a demeanor, if you sometimes say to yourself
in company—on entering a room, for instance—
Papa, potatoes, poultry, prunes and prism."

—Charles Dickens, English Writer (*Little Dorrit*)

Dryden may be properly considered as the father of English criticism, as the writer who first taught us to determine upon principles the merit of composition.

—Samuel Johnson, English Biographer and Lexicographer
(*The Lives of the Poets*)

MY HEART LEAPS UP WHEN I BEHOLD

A RAINBOW IN THE SKY:

SO WAS IT WHEN MY LIFE BEGAN;

SO IS IT NOW I AM A MAN;

SO BE IT WHEN I SHALL GROW OLD,

OR LET ME DIE!

THE CHILD IS FATHER OF THE MAN.

—William Wordsworth, English Romantic Poet ("My Heart Leaps Up")

Hath the rain a father? Or who hath begotten the drops of dew?

Out of whose womb came the ice? And the hoary frost of heaven, who hath gendered it?

—Job, Chapter 38, Verses 28–29 (The Bible)

Like as a father pitieth his children, so the Lord pitieth them that fear him.

—Psalm 103:13 (The Bible)

I THINK A CHILD SHOULD BE ALLOWED TO TAKE HIS FATHER'S OR MOTHER'S NAME AT WILL ON COMING OF AGE. PATERNITY IS A LEGAL FICTION.

—James Joyce, Irish Writer (Letter to His Brother Stanislaus)

Now he is himself paternal and these about him might be his sons. Who can say? The wise father knows his own child.

—James Joyce, Irish Writer (*Ulysses*)

This seems a fair deserving,
and must draw me

That which my father
loses; no less than all:

The younger rises when
the old doth fall.

—William Shakespeare, English Playwright (*King Lear*)

Lloyd George knew my father,
Father knew Lloyd George.

—Twentieth-Century English Folk Song

For me, by heaven, I bid you be assur'd,

I'll be your father and your brother too;

Let me but bear your love, I'll bear your cares.

—William Shakespeare, English Playwright (*Henry IV*)

I wish either my father or my mother, or indeed both of them, as they were in duty both equally bound to it, had minded what they were about when they begot me.

—Laurence Sterne, Irish Novelist
(The Life and Opinions of Tristram Shandy, Gentleman)

OUR FATHERS BROUGHT FORTH UPON THIS CONTINENT A NEW NATION, CONCEIVED IN LIBERTY, AND DEDICATED TO THE PROPOSITION THAT ALL MEN ARE CREATED EQUAL.

—Abraham Lincoln, Sixteenth President of the United States
(The Gettysburg Address)

There is no good father, that's the rule. Don't lay the blame on men but on the bond of paternity, which is rotten. To beget children, nothing better; to have them, what iniquity!

—Jean-Paul Sartre, French Philosopher (*The Words*)

*Father, dear father, come
home with me now,
The clock in the steeple strikes one.*

—Henry Clay Work, American Composer and Songwriter ("Come Home, Father")

The king is truly *parens patriae*, the
politique father of his people.

—James I, King of England (Spoken to Parliament)

Hence, vain deluding Joys,

The brood of Folly without father bred!

—John Milton, English Poet ("Il Penseroso")